Welcome to
Our Company
Your Office Manual

While You Were Out

PERSONNEL FILES

Welcome to
Our Company
Your Office Manual

Yolanda Nave

Workman Publishing, New York

DEDICATION

To my parents, Nick and Dorothy Nave

Copyright © 1988 by Yolanda Nave

Published simultaneously in Canada by
Saunders of Toronto Ltd.

Library of Congress Cataloging-in-Publication Data
Nave, Yolanda.
    Welcome to our company
    1. Business—Humor.   I. Title.
PN6231.B85N38   1988   741.5′ 973   88-40251
ISBN 0-89480-608-4 (pbk.)

Cover and book design: Kathleen Herlihy-Paoli

Workman Publishing Company, Inc.
708 Broadway
New York, NY 10003

Manufactured in the United States of America

First printing October 1988

10 9 8 7 6 5 4 3 2 1

Contents

Orientation

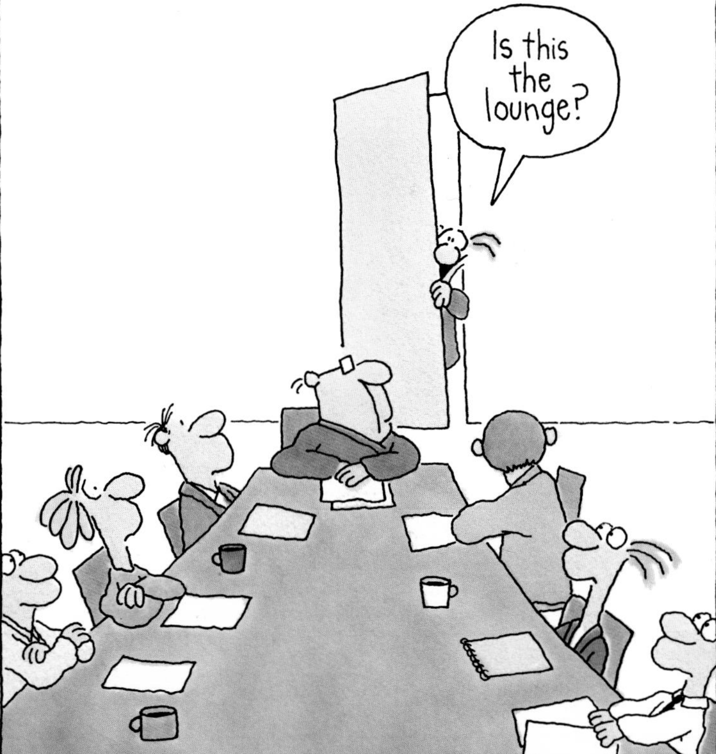

Congratulations!
You were selected for employment because you were the
best-qualified candidate, and because you met the
job-related requirements for the position.

As a rule, all new employees enter a three-month probationary period immediately upon employment.

Actually,
this is a get-acquainted
period.

It is also a time for training

. . . and acquiring new skills.

During this period the department head will review your performance

... and will offer guidance regarding your particular career path.

If at the end of the probationary period, both supervisor and employee are satisfied, the new employee is made welcome ...

and joins "The System."

Company
Policies

The Company is committed to the principle of fair and equitable treatment for all employees.

Our policies apply to everyone in the organization, without exception.

I. EQUAL OPPORTUNITY EMPLOYMENT

Employees are selected on the basis of skill and capability, without regard to age, race, sex, marital status, handicap, or national origin.

II. OFFICE HOURS

To accommodate all employees, office hours are flexible.

III. DRESS CODE

Dress is casual but professional, and always in good taste.

IV. PERSONAL PHONE CALLS

Personal telephone calls during business hours are
discouraged.

V. SMOKING

Smoking is permitted in designated areas only.

VI. CONFIDENTIALITY

Confidential Company information should not be improperly or accidentally disclosed.

VII. CODE OF ETHICS

Employees should observe a high standard of ethical conduct in all business activities.

VIII. SALARY ADMINISTRATION

Salaries are based on qualifications, and recognize individual differences in performance.

Salary adjustments are made periodically.

IX. PROMOTION POLICY

Whenever possible and practical, promotions are made from within the organization.

X. TRANSFER POLICY

Employees will be given reasonable advance notice of changes involving departmental transfers.

XI. CONFLICTS OF INTEREST

Activities that appear to be a conflict of interest should be avoided.

XII. "OPEN DOOR" POLICY

Employees are free to seek information and advice from management regarding their relationship with the Company

. . . or to call attention to any condition that appears to be operating to their disadvantage.

XIII. LEAVE POLICIES

Sick Leave is accrued over a one-year period at the rate of one half day per month.

Maternity Leave may be granted for a period of up to six weeks following childbirth.

Administrative Leave may be taken as necessary.

Bereavement Leave. All employees are allowed time off with pay in the event of a death in their family. The length of such leave may vary according to the circumstances.

Leave of Absence.

The Company and You

This section is intended as a guide to help you understand your responsibilities to Our Company

. . . and Our Company's responsibilities to you.

You have joined an organization where employees are helpful . . .

friendly...

and where working conditions are given careful attention by management.

The Company is actively interested in the continuing personal and professional development of each employee.

As a result, we provide an atmosphere that encourages professional advancement

. . . and job security.

COMPANY RULES

Attendance. Employees are expected to maintain a good record of attendance and punctuality.

Absences. In the case of unavoidable absence, please notify the office manager promptly.

Professional Image. Professional competence is often judged by external actions and appearances. Your conduct should reflect your professional posture at all times.

Office Security. If visitors or deliveries are expected, it is helpful to notify security personnel in advance.

Solicitations. To relieve employees of burdensome appeals, solicitation is limited to the annual drive for the Company's favorite charity.

Moonlighting. An employee may accept additional concurrent employment elsewhere, provided such employment does not impair job performance.

Disciplinary Action. Unsatisfactory work or violation of Company rules may result in disciplinary action.

Resignation or Termination. If you resign, Our Company requests that you give a minimum of two weeks' notice.

Likewise, in the event of termination you will be notified in advance.

Your Job

To protect Company interests, each employee is asked to sign an Employee Agreement.

Company people are also expected to follow established procedures . . .

and to respect the dignity of others.

While the job of a professional cannot be circumscribed by a rigid time schedule . . .

most assignments can be completed well within designated working hours.

There are, however, occasions or emergencies that necessitate overtime work.

We then expect that every employee will cooperate as needed.

For overtime hours actually worked, employees will receive satisfactory compensation.

When extensive overtime work is required, a full-time assistant will be provided.

EMPLOYEE RELATIONSHIPS

The very nature of the business invites disagreement at times.

Although most conflicts can be mutually resolved

. . . you may be called on to exercise considerable restraint.

It may be helpful to remember that your attitude is a key factor in evaluating your overall performance

. . . and carries considerable weight in determining your eligibility for a raise.

MEETINGS

Meetings are an important part of the work week, and should be considered as such by employees.

To avoid interruption, the weekly staff meeting will begin promptly at 7:45 every Monday morning.

From time to time you may be required to attend all-day meetings . . .

and brainstorming sessions.

Of course, some meetings are of a more personal nature.

OFFICES AND WORK AREAS

Work spaces are assigned by management

. . . and include such considerations as space planning and layout . . .

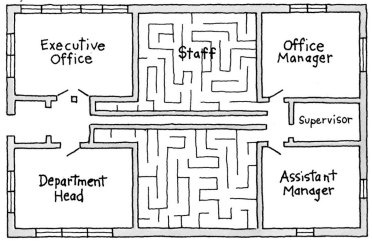

comfort . . .

and decor.

Alterations to existing office areas require prior approval from management.

To the extent possible, offices should be clear or neat at the close of business each day.

OFFICE EQUIPMENT AND SUPPLIES

Office equipment is to be used for business purposes only.

Supply requisitions are filled routinely at 10:00 a.m. and 3:00 p.m.

MAIL

Outgoing. A postage meter is provided for routine mailings. Employees may purchase stamps for personal use.

Incoming. All correspondence addressed to employees will be promptly distributed.

SAFETY

Each employee is expected to report any condition that may appear to be hazardous.

HOUSEKEEPING

Housekeeping rules are posted in the kitchen area.

LOST AND FOUND

All found articles should be turned over to the supervisor, where such may be claimed upon proper identification.

Benefits

HOLIDAYS

Our Company observes seven holidays per year.

BONUS PLAN

All employees will receive a Christmas bonus.

PROFIT-SHARING PLAN

The Profit-Sharing Plan allows all eligible employees
to benefit financially from Our Company's profitability.

VACATIONS

Vacations are provided annually for all permanent employees.

After 5 years, an employee becomes eligible for 3 weeks' vacation.

RETIREMENT BENEFITS

After 25 years, employees are eligible for early retirement.

And for all those who persevere—

EMPLOYEE ASSISTANCE PLAN

The EAP provides assistance for employees who are having performance, attendance, or work behavior problems caused by stress. Warning signs of stress include:

Drastic Change in Personality

Avoidance of Coworkers

Confusion

Hostility

Unusual Lack of Energy

Inappropriate Dress or Appearance

When a sustained decline in job performance is observed . . .

the employee is referred to management for confidential guidance and counseling.

If symptoms persist, see the Company doctor

. . . or seek other professional advice.

In addition to our excellent benefits package, the Company provides recreational activities for your enjoyment. Employees are encouraged to enroll in our Health & Fitness Program

. . . and to participate in Company-sponsored sports activities, including volleyball, golf, bowling, and tennis.

The Company's Annual Picnic is an employee favorite. All employees and their families are invited.

Weekend retreats provide a change of pace and improve morale. Attendance is mandatory.

Whether you were with us in the beginning or today marks the start of your career here, we wish you much success and happiness.

THANKS TO:

Edite Kroll

Suzanne Rafer

Anne Kostick

Peter Workman

Kathleen Herlihy-Paoli

Toumonava Nave
Jane Russ
Bobby Drinnon
William A. Fitzhugh III
Tondalayo Strong
Nathan Howard
Angie Murray
Lisa Huskey